BOOK ANALYSIS

Written by Florence Hellin
Translated by Carly Probert

AF131351

The Just Assassins

BY ALBERT CAMUS

Bright
≡Summaries.com

ALBERT CAMUS

FRENCH WRITER, PLAYWRIGHT, ESSAYIST AND PHILOSOPHER

- **Born in Mondovi (Algeria) in 1913**
- **Died in Villeblevin in 1960**
- **Notable works:**
  - *The Stranger* (1942), novel
  - *The Myth of Sisyphus* (1942), essay
  - *The Plague* (1947), novel

A Frenchman born in Algeria and Nobel Prize winner, Albert Camus (1913-1960) is one of the major writers of the twentieth century. A politically committed individual, philosopher, journalist, playwright and novelist, he left his mark on his era with his reflection on absurdism, which he nuanced and made more sensitive and humane.

Widely admired, and sometimes criticized, Camus received considerable attention worldwide with his novels *The Plague* (1947) and, in particular, *The Stranger* (1942). He died prematurely in 1960 as a result of a car crash.

THE JUST ASSASSINS

A PLAY OF REFUSAL AND DENUNCIATION

- **Genre:** play
- **Reference edition:** Camus, A. (1985) *The Just Assassins*. Trans. Cagney, J. New York: Hunter College.
- **First edition:** 1949
- **Themes:** attack, death, Russian revolution, loyalty, rebellion, history

The Just Assassins is a play in five acts, performed for the first time in 1949. It belongs to the "Cycle of Revolt" with *The Plague* (1947) and *The Rebel* (1951). The goal of this cycle is the rejection and denunciation of all forms of totalitarianism. For *The Just Assassins*, Camus took inspiration from an event of the Russian revolution: in January 1905, in Moscow, a group of terrorists linked to the revolutionary socialist party organized an attack on the Grand Duke Serge. This attack, and the preceding circumstances, is the object of the play, with engagement as the central notion.

SUMMARY

This tragic play is made up of five acts. It tells of the preparation for an attack against the Grand Duke of Russia, Serge. The first attempt is a failure, but the second fulfills its goal. The revolutionary is arrested and sentenced to death.

PREPARING FOR THE ATTACK

In an apartment, the assault group of the Organization, which regroups the socialist revolutionaries, gathers in order to prepare an attack against the Grand Duke Serge, the symbol of the despotic power that was alienating Russia ("We will kill that murderer", Act 1).

Boris Annenkov, the group's leader, is a moderate and calm man. It is he who makes all the decisions concerning the attack. He has under his orders a team of several people:

- Dora, a meticulous young woman, is in charge of the fabrication of bombs;
- Stepan is seen as a terrorist without any moral sense. His return after three years in prison and in hiding is nonetheless applauded by Boris and Dora;
- Alexis is a young revolutionary who is unsure of himself and full of doubts;
- Yanek is a sensitive and idealist man.

Everything is ready, the attack is supposed to take place the following day. Those who will launch the bombs have already been designated: Yanek Kaliayev will throw the first bomb, Alexis Voinov the second one, if the first were to fail.

The first meeting between Stepan and Kaliayev is stormy: they both have different ideas about the action and the fight they are engaged in. Stepan openly declares his mistrust in Yanek, nicknamed "the poet" because of his sensitivity. He wants to throw the bomb instead of Yanek, but Annenkov refuses. On his side, Yanek is assured of the unrelenting support of Dora, his beloved.

THE ATTACK

The next evening, in the same apartment, Dora and Annenkov watch the street and wait for the explosion. The tension heightens their respective anxiousness. Far away, the noise of the Grand Duke's carriage is heard, and is followed by silence. Not hearing the explosion, Dora is convinced that Yanek has been arrested. She is verging on despair. Voinov arrives quickly afterwards. He knows nothing of what happened, as he was waiting for the first bomb explosion in order to be able to launch his own.

A few moments later, Yanek comes into the room, crying. He could not throw the bomb, not because he was afraid, but because there were children in the Grand Duke's carriage, namely the latter's nephews. The young man, aghast, puts the decision to the other members of the group. If they decide that the attack must happen despite the children's presence, he will launch the bomb.

Annenkov, Vionov and Dora support him. As for Stepan, he is furious and does not share their opinion ("When we decide to forget about children, that day we'll be masters of the world and the revolution will triumph", Act 2). Stepan's antagonism towards Yanek reaches its peak. Finally, they all agree that the Organization cannot kill innocent children. The attack is therefore delayed until the next day.

At the same place, two days later, all the members of the group are present before the second attempt. Voinov talks to Annenkov privately: he announces that he will not launch his bomb, as he doesn't have the courage to do so. He would rather continue the struggle in the comities, using propaganda. Annenkov therefore decides to take his place, while Stepan will replace him as the leader for as long as necessary.

Dora and Yanek enjoy their last moments of intimacy. After their parting, the revolutionaries split up. Stepan and Dora remain alone at the apartment. The clock strikes seven. The noise of the Grand Duke's carriage come closer then fades away. An explosion resounds. The Grand Duke Serge is dead.

THE ARREST

Yanek Kaliayev, who has been found, is imprisoned. A guard and a prisoner, Foka, enter his cell. Foka has his sentence shortened by one year for every prisoner he hangs. This is how Yanek meets his future executioner.

Then comes Skoutarov, the director of the police department. He wants to offer Yanek mercy on the condition that he turns in his accomplices. The revolutionary refuses. After this second visit, it is the Grand Duchess's turn to meet him.

She intends to crack him. She wants the one who killed her husband to confess and live to be considered a murderer.

After the Grand Duchess's departure, Skoutarov comes back: he announces that he will publish Kaliayev's confession, proof of his treason, the next day. Yanek refuses, preferring death to disloyalty towards his companions and the idea they defend.

One week later, in another apartment, the group, minus Yanek, is gathered again. Annenkov, Dora, Stepan and Voinov wonder about their comrade's attitude. They wait to hear whether he has been executed or not. Stepan and Voinov go looking for information: Yanek has been executed and therefore has not betrayed them. Torn by grief, Dora decides to be the one who launches the next bomb, in order to be hanged with the same rope as her lover.

CHARACTER STUDY

YANEK KALIAYEV

He is nicknamed the poet, because of his sensitivity, his spontaneity and his enthusiasm. Annenkov, convinced of his value, has given him the task of throwing the first bomb. However, his hand was unable to perform the fatal act because there were children in the Grand Duke's carriage. For the second attack, he did not hesitate, proving his courage and determination.

Kaliayev has all the qualities of a "good revolutionary": he is able to be nimble, efficient, and discreet. However, he is an atypical terrorist. Above all, he loves happiness and beauty, which is why he wants to put an end to despotism. The aim of his action is to give life a chance. He is prepared to kill in order to build a better world, where nobody will kill anymore, if he believes that the idea he defends is just. It is not hate which is at the center of his struggle, but love. Instead of blindly obeying the principles and orders of the Organization, he values his personal ethics (which is why he does not launch the bomb on the Grand duke's nephews, nor does he denounce his companions). He represents Camus' idea of engagement.

STEPAN FEDOROV

He has come back to the Organization after three years of prison and hiding. This experience has made him bitter. From his first meeting with Kaliayev, he treats him with disdain, thinking him too passionate and too fiery, too much of a 'poet'.

Stepan is the opposite of Kaliayev: he is a true terrorist. He is rigid and obeys the orders of the Organization to the letter. He has neither morals nor conscience. In his opinion, the end justifies the means, even if innocent blood will be shed. Hatred and anger are the motors behind his actions.

However, this coldness and austerity are the result of deep wounds. When he finds himself alone with Dora, he shows her the scars left by the torture he endured in prison, and reveals his weaknesses and secret flaws: "All these years of fighting, of agony, traitors, prison…and to cap it off, this. (He shows his marks.) Where would I find the energy to love? I barely have enough to hate. That's better than not feeling anything" (Act 3). His last thought concerning Kaliayev is revealing: "I envied him" (Act 5).

DORA DOUBLEDOV

Kaliayev's beloved, Dora is the only female character of importance. She has been in the Organization for three years. Meticulous and a perfectionist, she is the one in charge of making the bombs.

More than the other characters, the young woman reminisces about the life she led before joining the group and its clandestine activities: "I remember back when I was a student. I laughed. I was pretty then. I spent hours walking and dreaming" (Act 3).

In the moments when Kaliayev gets carried away by his enthusiasm and passion, she brings him back to reality. For example, she reminds him of the fact that the Grand Duke is still a human being, and that to commit an attack is to die twice.

Through her presence and her listening skills, she invites the others to confide in her (particularly Annenkov and Stepan).

Dora's love for Yanek is unconditional. She defends him vehemently when he is attacked by Stepan and she supports his choices and decisions. From time to time, however, she doubts the love Yanek has for her: "Do you love me more than justice, more than the Organization? (...)You didn't answer me. Just tell me, would you love me if I weren't in the Organization?" (Act 3). Upon hearing of her lover's death, in a moment between despair and folly, the young woman decides to avenge his death: she will be the one throwing the next bomb. This ultimate proof of love will unite her in death with her lover.

BORIS ANNENKOV

Boris Annenkov is the group's leader. He makes the decisions concerning the attack. It is namely he who chooses the people who are going to launch the bombs.

He is calm man, who mediates the conflicts between Yanek and Stepan. He appears as a moderate leader: "I cannot let you say that everything is allowed" (Act 2).

During his discussion with Dora, he unveils his personality

He is aware that his status as leader protects him: "It's convenient, after all, to be forced not to actually throw the bomb." (Act 2) He escapes this security by stepping in to replace Voinov for the second attack, and with this decision, his courage is put on the same scale as Yanek.

Sometimes, he thinks about the life he used to live and about the sacrifices he had to make in the name of the idea he defends. Thus, he is not an inflexible and imperturbable leader: he has his moments of doubts and sagging. He regains his leadership qualities by making decisions for the group and wishing to be on the field with Yanek.

ALEXIS VOINOV

Alexis Voinov is a former university student who has been sent back for having said something negative about the Tsar. At the beginning of the play, he is determined, sure of his beliefs, ready to throw the fatal bomb.

After the failure of the first attack, he starts to doubt his actions. He remains faithful to the idea in its essence, but does not feel able to be on the front line. He is not ready for terror. He is afraid of throwing the bomb and ashamed for feeling that way. He will continue his engagement, but in the domain of propaganda. This is just as risky, but at least, you do not have to see what happens (Act 3).

Alexis, more than Dora and Annenkov, represents the doubts and fears scattered across the path of a revolutionary. After Yanek's arrest, he comes back to the group, carried by a new surge of courage. He wishes to occupy the place left vacant by Yanek and to continue launching bombs. Thus, Yanek's example gives him the force and courage to fight on the front line: "We must support him with our pride, the way he supported us with his example" (Act 5). His action, once questioned, will never be doubted again. He, in turn wants to be an example for those who will follow.

ANALYSIS

The Just Assassins is a play defined by a double context: the context against which the play is set, namely Russia in 1905, and the context in which it was written, in 1949.

The Russian Revolution of 1905

Russia began the 20th century in an anarchic atmosphere of terrorism and violence: it was oppressed by the Tsar Nicolas II's autocracy (a form of government where the sovereign grants himself unlimited power). Attempts at overthrowing the regime were numerous, and various anarchic cells appeared. Very early on, a schism appeared inside the opposition movement: Some condemned the excess of violence, while others advocated hard terrorism.

Insurrection is in the air. In January 1905, a mass of demonstrators went to the Winter Palace, where the Tsar was supposed to be, to give him a petition. But the latter had gone, giving free reign to the police force. The crowd was slaughtered. In February of the same year, the Grand Duke Serge was assassinated in a bomb attack, by a man called Ivan Platonovich Kalyayev, a member of the revolutionary socialist Fighters. Following this attack, tragic events took place increasingly often: strikes, mutinies, murders, etc.

Camus took a deep interest in the actors of this revolution. In his work, we find familiar-sounding names: Yanek Kaliayev, Dora Brilliant, Boris Savinkov, etc. The frame of the real history has also been followed: the first attack was a failure due to the presence of children in the Grand Duke's carriage. The final attack was a blood bath and the details given by the Grand Duchess in the play correspond to those given by the newspapers at the time.

The post-war context

The Just Assassins was performed for the first time in 1949, four years after the end of the Second World War. However, another conflict seemed imminent at the time, that of the Cold War (1947-1990). Tensions between East and West are indeed latent. Barely recovered from the brown plague, Western Europe had to face communism and the expansionist desires of the Soviet Union. The same year, the NATO was created. This troubled period led Camus to think about the notions of political action and engagement.

Therefore, *The Just Assassins*, because of its theme and context, is a work inscribed in the debates of its time. While Europe recovered with difficulty from the damages of war and the attacks against its democratic ideals, the intellectuals took position on international policy topics, such as the Indochina War (1946-1954), American Imperialism and Soviet expansionism. The Russian event which inspired Camus was echoed in the European political situation after the war: in both cases, men were taking a stance against political systems and socio-economic situations which they judged unbearable and inacceptable. The main question was how to go from an engagement or a revolt to an efficient action.

Jean-Paul Sartre (1905-1980) was a French philosopher and writer. He is as well-known for his literary and philosophical work as for his political engagement. Existentialism, for which he became the main representative, permeates his works. This philosophy states the total responsibility of man, whose actions are not pre-determined and who is master of his own destiny. An engaged intellectual, radical left-wing adherent (member of the communist party for a time), Sartre fought on all the frontlines: Algerian War, Cuban revolution, Israeli-Palestinian conflict, etc.

His works, both literary (*Nausea, No Exit*) and philosophical (*Being and Nothingness, Existentialism is a Humanism*) are still widely read and discussed.

The Just Assassins is an answer to his play *Dirty hands*. In these two plays, the authors discuss the notion of engagement and the relation between ethics and practice.

TWO DIFFERENT NOTIONS OF ACTION

Throughout the play, the personalities of Kaliayev and Stepan oppose each other. Through these characters, Camus presents two different theses on engagement:

- Stepan represents the absolute submission to revolutionary duty. The first duty is to obey the orders of the

Organization. One must act, and all the means are good, regardless of the stakes and consequences. He accepts the deaths: "We are murderers and we have chosen to be." (Act 2). The end justifies the means, whatever they may be.

- Camus does not share this opinion (Stepan is isolated and unsupported). This vision is closer to what Sartre says, with the two authors opposing one another about the means engagement can take; Jean-Paul Sartre was unwilling to make the slightest concession concerning revolutionary engagement;

- Kaliayev embodies disobedience to the revolutionary norms, in the name of ethics and values. He bears in minds the innocence of the victims and the horror that would result from such a crime. Kaliayev keeps his humanity and chooses not to become a tormentor himself. In his fight against a system and in favor of an idea, he acts not as an assassin, but as a defender of justice. Kaliayev has not chosen the crime. The situation in which he finds himself has driven him to it. He represents engagement as Camus wishes it to be. It is a thought-through and not a blind engagement, as he is able to discern the limits of his action and to adapt to circumstances.

A VISION OF POLITICAL MURDER

The origin of *The Just Assassins* is based on a reflection on what a political murder is. This reflection is both political and metaphysical.

- Political: Can a revolutionary kill? If he can kill, in what conditions and what are the limits? Does the end justify the means? In answering these questions, the characters understand the difference between the ideal of justice and the reality on the field. On the one hand, they act in the name of idealism: they struggle for better conditions of life, to give life a chance. On the other hand, they realize that revolution and justice cannot be obtained through a spiritual revolution: blood must be shed, including their own.

- The terrorist action is therefore necessary, yet it has its limitations: it should be targeted, as innocents should not be sacrificed. The characters have a sense of honor. They commit an injustice to create justice, they deprive themselves of happiness to give others a chance to experience it. If the revolutionaries do not act, they warrant tragedy. Whether they kill or not, they are guilty.

- Metaphysical: The group has taken on a mission that is deeper than simple politics. The characters become kinds of prophets and the bomb replaces the prediction. Their actions are beyond activism. They want to recreate a society where justice and love are sovereign. They are martyrs out of vocation: death is inescapable. Any other type of action would be useless. Death is the instrument of their salvation and glorification. Through his death, Kaliayev enters the ranks of the heroes and becomes a legend.

FURTHER REFLECTION

SOME QUESTIONS TO THINK ABOUT...

- This play belongs to the "Cycle of Revolt", as does *The Plague* and *The Rebel*. What are the similarities between these three works?
- Explain the title of this play, *The Just Assassins*.
- In your opinion, why did Camus chose the Russian Revolution of 1905 as the context of his play?
- Relate this play to the political context in which Camus wrote it.
- What is Dora's role, as the only woman in the play?
- "The end justifies the means". Comment on this quotation taken from the play.
- What form of engagement does Camus promote and how does he make this known in his work? How does he differ from Sartre?
- How is *The Just Assassins* a response to Sartre's play *Dirty Hands*?
- Even though Yanek tries to be just, he sheds blood. Is this acceptable? Can a revolution be pacifist?
- How does political murder have a metaphysical dimension?
- Are the themes discussed in *The Just Assassins* still topical? Justify your answer using examples.

We want to hear from you!
Leave a comment on your online library
and share your favourite books on social media!

FURTHER READING

REFERENCE EDITION

- Camus, A. (1985) *The Just Assassins*. Trans. Cagney, J. New York: Hunter College.

REFERENCE STUDIES

- Guérin, J.-Y. ed. (2009) *Dictionnaire Albert Camus*. Paris: Robert Laffont.

MORE FROM BRIGHTSUMMARIES.COM

- Reading guide - *The Plague* by Albert Camus
- Reading guide - *The Stranger* by Albert Camus
- Reading guide – *The Fall* by Albert Camus
- Reading guide – *The First Man* by Albert Camus
- Reading guide – *The Myth of Sisyphus* by Albert Camus

www.brightsummaries.com

Ebook EAN: 9782806270399

Paperback EAN: 9782806272850

Legal Deposit: D/2015/12603/580

Cover: © Primento

Digital conception by Primento, the digital partner of publishers.